The Stubborn Texan Volume I:

What the U.S. Constitution Really Says (And What it Doesn't)

By Clay Harrison

CLAY HARRISON

Copyright © 2017 Clay Harrison

All rights reserved.

To my lovely wife Tara:

the most stubborn Texan of all

Contents

Preface

Chapter 1: Conservatives and Moderns

Chapter 2: The Founding of the Republic

Chapter 3: Tension Among Giants

Chapter 4: Freedom of Religion

Chapter 5: Freedom of Speech

Chapter 6: Freedom of the Press

Chapter 7: Redefining Marriage

Chapter 8: Abortion

Conclusion

Appendix

About the Author

Notes

Preface

I'm a Christian and a Conservative. I'm a husband, a soon-to-be father, and a son. I'm a military veteran and a criminal prosecutor and a lifelong Texan. All of these facts shape how I view the world. In the courtroom, these would be called my biases.

I write as an attorney with a decade of legal experience. I'm not an expert in Constitutional Law, but I know enough to walk you through the minefields. I also write as veteran of Operation Enduring Freedom. I was never a combat soldier, but my experience as an Air Force JAG and as a special operations lawyer taught me how to get enough information to make the right decision, how to process conflicting data, and how to find order in the midst of apparent chaos.

Most of the people I know are a lot like me. They care about doing what's right, taking care of their families, and pursuing happiness along the way. They are not filled with hate, fear, or pride. They are not racist or sexist or bigoted. They are not narrow-minded or backwards.

I know these things to be true beyond doubt. However, at this moment in American history, everything I've said is open to question. A growing segment of the population has its doubts about Conservatives today. Dominant news networks, outspoken celebrities, and many influential government figures are all voicing the same misgivings about us:

"You voted for who? Why are you so intolerant?"

"You believe in what? Why are you so narrow-minded?"

A husband who says he believes in traditional marriage is accused of hating gay people. A mother who wants her daughter to be free to pray at her graduation ceremony is told to stop forcing her religion on other people's children. A restaurant owner who believes that the federal government should stick to coining money and stay out of his bathrooms is condemned for being "The New Jim Crow."[1]

We live in a world who sees itself as marching forward under the banner of progress. We agree that it is marching, but to us it appears to be stumbling around in well-worn circles. They reject us because in their eyes, we are backwards, fanatical, and self-righteous. I don't expect to win many converts with this short book. Instead, I merely write to explain what I believe and why. Perhaps it will strengthen the reader's convictions, as it is the singular goal of this book.

It is certainly easier to point out what Conservatives disagree with than it is to explain what we agree upon. We are quick to pronounce what we stand against, but what do we stand for?

If this book is to be worthwhile, it will be sufficiently narrow in scope. I don't intend to take on arguments in this short piece that require large volumes to examine. I don't pretend to be an expert and I won't attempt to write for the first time what greater minds than my own have already accomplished.

I believe there's an itch that needs to be scratched. While popular culture of the U.S. has consistently marched to the political left, Americans are center-right. If you saw the red and blue map from the 2016 Presidential election, it's hard to disagree.

This is not a book about people. Instead, it is a book about ideas. Every person has tremendous value, whether they agree with me or take a different view. As C.S. Lewis reminds us in The Weight of Glory, while empires and governments will all fall away, every person we meet is of eternal importance:

> "It is in the light of these overwhelming possibilities, it is with the awe and the circumspection proper to them, that we should conduct all of our dealings with one another, all friendships, all loves, all play, all politics. There are no ordinary people. You have never talked to a mere mortal.
>
> Nations, cultures, arts, civilizations - these are mortal, and their life is to ours as the life of a gnat. But it is

> immortals whom we joke with, work with, marry, snub, and exploit - immortal horrors or everlasting splendors."[2]

With this book, I intend to defend and fortify some ideas while attacking and dismantling others. I have no such plans against men and women. My subjects are beliefs, arguments, and ideas, but never people.

I've earnestly tried to avoid an "Us vs. Them" tone throughout this book. At this critical task, I'm sure I've failed miserably. I know people who will disagree with much of what I've written, in substance and in tone. Some are tremendous, intelligent, and kind people. If offense is taken, I can promise that it was never my intent or desire.

Chapter One:
Conservatives and Moderns

The words in these chapters will probably strike various people in different ways. This might even land on the bookshelves of a few easy-to-please Conservatives. For those on the political left, however, the only question is whether these pages will better serve in a fireplace or next to the toilet. I suppose that depends on the ply-count of the paper, but that is out of my hands unfortunately.

I take the Conservative view of government, and I'll refer to it as such. On the other hand, giving a name to its primary opposing viewpoint can be tricky. Some writers use "Liberal" or "Progressive." Some mix-and-match along the way. Instead of using these terms, I've chosen instead to counter the Conservative view with the Modern view. Let me explain why.

First of all, I won't be using "Republican" and "Democrat." Not all Democrats agree with Modern ideas. Many lifelong Democrats even reject key statements in the Democratic platform. It's entirely possible to be a Conservative Democrat, as we've seen in Texas. On the other hand, it's possible to be a Republican, Libertarian, or Independent whose beliefs have been watered down and diluted with the Modern gospel.

"Liberal" is a word I've tried to avoid because the meaning keeps changing. For most of my arguments, I'll refer to the writings of famous old dead people. Sometimes it's the Founding Fathers in America, the great thinkers of Europe, or the philosophers of Ancient Greece. The term "Liberal" used to mean something completely different than it does today. British writer G.K. Chesterton proudly called himself a Liberal, but his ideas are decidedly Conservative by today's standards. I've also shamelessly stolen his use of the term "Modern" from his book <u>Orthodoxy</u>, in which he said,

> "I know that some moderns are asking to have their wives chosen by scientists, and they may soon be asking, for all I know, to have their noses blown by nurses … In short, the democratic faith is this: that the most terribly important things must be left to ordinary men themselves—the mating of the sexes, the rearing of the young, the laws of the state. This is democracy; and in this I have always believed."[3]

I will not use the term "Progressive" unless it is absolutely necessary. It implies Progressive ideas are leading us towards "progress." While I agree that these ideas move us in a direction, I don't believe the direction happens to be forward.

Conservatives believe in limited government while Moderns want expanded federal power. Conservatives hate political correctness while Moderns push for censorship of ideas they deem to be bigoted and hateful.

Conservatives believe in natural law; the idea that men and women were created with an internal moral compass of right and wrong. It's why Conservatives in America tend to be Christians or at least believe in God.

Modern views, on the other hand, are founded largely on moral relativism and the idea that laws come from society and not from God. Belief in a non-judgmental, generic spirituality is common.

Conservatives believe America is a great nation where anyone can succeed based on hard work, common sense, and a little good fortune. Moderns argue that America is systemically racist, sexist, homophobic and bigoted, and that straight people, white people, and males are privileged.

I've also chosen the term "Modern" because I believe it captures the spirit of the contemporary attack on Conservative values. It isn't that Modern ideas are new. In fact, most Modern views are leftover, rejected ideas from hundreds of years ago. Rather, our age, like every other age, wants to believe the newest ideas are the best ideas in the same way that the newest iPhone technology is the best iPhone technology. However, the undeniable progress of technology is a far different thing from the dubious "progress" of morality. Consider how man uses the newest technologies to reign terror upon his fellow man.

While new ideas can be truly good, it's important to keep them in their proper place. On this, C.S. Lewis has this to say:

> **"We all need the books that will correct the characteristic mistakes of our own period. And that means the old books... We may be sure that the characteristic blindness of the twentieth century lies where we have never suspected it. None of us can fully escape this blindness."[4]**

In a hundred years, the ideas I've described as Modern are likely to have been abandoned and replaced with yet a more "advanced" value system. I believe the characteristic blindness of our moment in American history is best captured by the Modern gospel. It is this system of values, beliefs, and ideas that I have chosen to confront.

Chapter Two:

<u>The Founding of the Republic</u>

Before we look at the actual words of the Constitution, we should understand the historic events that led to its creation. Most of us remember from school that America was once a British colony. In fact, while early Americans had to pay taxes to the Crown, they had very little control over their own government. The first Americans were self-reliant farmers, and this is crucial to understanding their mindset. If they didn't work hard, they starved to death.

On the other hand, the land of opportunity presented limitless possibilities. Built into the American character was a hard work ethic and respect for the private ownership of land. Today we consider these to be qualities of the American Middle Class.

Conflict with the British over taxes and government eventually came to a head, sparking what we now refer to as The Revolutionary War or The War for American Independence. From 1775 to 1783, American rebels fought the British redcoats by land and by sea.

On July 4, 1776, the Founding Fathers signed the Declaration of Independence. While victory in a military sense was still a long way off, this document made the case for war and was written publicly to the world. Consider these words:

"When in the course of human events it becomes necessary for one people to dissolve the political bands which have connected them with another and to assume among the powers of the earth, the separate and equal station to which the laws of nature and of nature's God entitle them, a decent respect to the opinions of mankind requires that they should declare the causes which impel them to the separation.[5]

[Simplified translation: Americans feel that it's necessary to explain to the world our reasons for declaring independence from Britain.]

We hold these truths to be self-evident, that all men are created equal, that they are endowed by their Creator with certain unalienable Rights, that among these are Life, Liberty and the pursuit of Happiness.

[Simplified translation: When God created us, he gave every man's life meaning and value. Our rights are not from man or society but from God himself.]

That to secure these rights, governments are instituted among

men, deriving their just powers from the consent of the governed, That whenever any form of government becomes destructive of these ends, it is the right of the people to alter or to abolish it, and to institute new government, laying its foundation on such principles and organizing its powers in such form, as to them shall seem most likely to effect their safety and happiness…"

[Simplified translation: God is not to serve governments. Instead, governments are God's tool for administering justice among men. If the government fails at this, it should be replaced.]

As military victory was approaching in 1781, the Founding Fathers ratified the Articles of Confederation. This document created a "confederacy" or loosely bound alliance of thirteen independent American colonies. The over-arching federal government was very weak and had to ask permission of individual colonies before doing much of anything. Think of the modern day United Nations. It was effectively a paper tiger.

The need for a better system was apparent, but Americans disagreed on what to do about it. They were divided into two groups. On one side were the Federalists who wanted a robust national government with significant power over the states. On the other side were the Anti-Federalists who wanted a more constrained federal government with strong independent states.

The Federalists believed America would be unable to defend itself if a major war broke out with a foreign power. Thirteen independent armies and navies would be much less effective than one unified military. They also wanted the federal government to have an unlimited power of taxation, a view that was a great source of friction.

Additionally, the colonies were doing harm to the national economy by waging trade warfare against one another. For example, they imposed high import taxes on goods from other colonies. The Federalists intended to address all of these problems with a powerful national government that regulated the military, foreign affairs, taxes, and interstate commerce.

However, the Anti-Federalists were not so quick to establish a powerful sovereign government. They had just fought a bloody war to gain independence from one tyrant overseas and were not excited about the prospect of creating a new king on this side of the Atlantic Ocean.

In a superb example of Americans engaging one another in the "Marketplace of Ideas," a topic we'll discuss later, the two sides respectfully debated one another in the newspapers. They traded arguments and exchanged points and counterpoints in the public eye.

They did not take offense when someone disagreed with them. They did not censor one another or attempt to silence countering voices through violence, intimidation, or hurt feelings. Instead, both sides argued their cases in the hope that they might reach a compromise, and they did.

The Constitution was ratified in 1788, replacing the Articles of Confederation. The federal government did gain a lot of influence, but with significant limits. These checks on federal power came primarily through the first ten amendments. The Bill of Rights, as these amendments came to be known, restrained the national government in major ways and protected the freedoms of individual Americans.

Contained in the first ten amendments are the following rights:

Freedom of Religion, Freedom of Speech, Freedom of the Press, the Right to Bear Arms, and the Right to Counsel in criminal cases, just to name a few.

A fitting way to close this chapter on the founding of the American Republic is to hear the prayer of Benjamin Franklin delivered to the Constitutional Convention on June 28, 1787.

> **"Mr. President, the small progress we have made after four or five weeks**

close attendance and continual reasonings with each other -- our different sentiments on almost every question, several of the last producing as many no's as aye's, is methinks a melancholy proof of the imperfection of the human understanding. We indeed seem to feel our own wont of political wisdom, since we have been running about in search of it. We have gone back to ancient history for models of government, and examined the different forms of those republics which having been formed with the seeds of their own dissolution now no longer exist. And we have viewed modern states all round Europe, but find none of their Constitutions suitable to our circumstances..."[6]

[Simplified translation: Our arguing and squabbling with one another is proof of the limits of human wisdom. In search of political guidance, we have studied the histories of other republics. However, nothing exactly fits our case.]

"In this situation of this assembly groping as it were in the dark to find political truth, and scarce able to distinguish it when to us, how has it happened, sir, that we have not hitherto once thought of humbly applying to the Father of Lights to illuminate our understandings? In the beginning of the contest with Great Britain, when we were sensible of danger we had daily prayer in this room for the divine protection. Our prayers, sir, were heard, and they were graciously answered. All of us who were engaged in the struggle must have observed frequent instances of a superintending Providence in our favor. To that kind Providence we owe this happy opportunity of consulting in peace on the means of establishing our future national felicity. And have we now forgotten that powerful friend? Or do we imagine that we no longer need His assistance..."

[Simplified translation: When war broke out, we prayed to God for protection and He answered our prayers. Let' s not forget Him now. God's hand has been on us from the beginning and He will not forsake us now.]

"I have lived, Sir, a long time and the

longer I live, the more convincing proofs I see of this truth -- that God governs in the affairs of men. And if a sparrow cannot fall to the ground without his notice, is it probable that an empire can rise without his aid? We have been assured, sir, in the sacred writings that "except the Lord build they labor in vain that build it." I firmly believe this; and I also believe that without his concurring aid we shall succeed in this political building no better than the builders of Babel: We shall be divided by our little partial local interests; our projects will be confounded, and we ourselves shall become a reproach and a bye word down to future age. And what is worse, mankind may hereafter this unfortunate instance, despair of establishing governments by human wisdom, and leave it to chance, war, and conquest..."

[Simplified translation: If we build this republic on our own with only human wisdom, it will fall apart and we will be remembered as a failure in the history books. If we are to have any hope of success, we must commit our plans to

God.]

"I therefore beg leave to move -- that henceforth prayers imploring the assistance of Heaven, and its blessings on our deliberations, be held in this assembly every morning before we proceed to business, and that one or more of the clergy of this city be requested to officiate in that service..."

[Simplified translation: Let's make a practice of praying together before we begin working on the Constitution each day.]

Chapter Three:

Tension Among Giants

While the Federalists pushed for a mighty national government, they too had their concerns about being dominated by an all-powerful Ruler-King. They were familiar with Lord Acton's warning, "Power tends to corrupt, and absolute power corrupts absolutely."

The Constitution divides the federal government into three co-equal branches: Legislative, Executive, and Judiciary. To prevent any one branch from overwhelming and overpowering the others, the Constitution establishes a system of checks and balances. It is a Divinely inspired, ingenious, brilliant system that is at the same time impractical, maddening, and almost unworkable to its practitioners. It was designed that way.

Imagine if the three branches were giants. One giant's leg is chained to another's arm and that one's arm is chained to the third's forehead. This is why at least one author has referred to it as the "blessed pains of checks and balances."[7] It is not efficient, but it was never supposed to be. Instead, it was designed to prevent a small group of people from running roughshod over the rest of the country, imposing the values of a few on millions of Americans.

The Anti-Federalists signed off on the Constitution only because the Bill of Rights, which included the 10th

Amendment, was ratified as well. Here's exactly what it says:

> "The powers not delegated to the United States by the Constitution, nor prohibited by it to the states, are reserved to the states respectively, or to the people."

What the 10th Amendment says is that there are two types of powers: those that belong to the federal government and those that belong to the state and local governments. If it belongs to the federal government, it is named in the Constitution. If it isn't mentioned, then it belongs to the state and local governments.

The 10th Amendment works like a person's will upon their death. Imagine if a widow dies and her lawyer reads the document to the lady's surviving relatives:

> "My house and my land go to my children. The rest of my property goes to my church."

If the lady's will were translated into "Constitutional language," then it would sound like this:

> "I delegate my house and my land to my children. The rest of my property is reserved to my church."

So then, who owns the green tractor in the pasture? Who

gets the money in the bank and the stocks and bonds and all the rest? Because these things were not delegated expressly to the children, they are thereby reserved to the church.

The Constitution delegates the following powers to the federal government: the power to tax, to coin money, to establish post offices and roads, to issue patents for inventions, to establish a federal court system, to raise a national military, to declare war, to regulate interstate commerce, and to conduct diplomacy with other nations.

The Constitution reserves the following powers to the states: pretty much everything else. In the words of James Madison,

> **"The powers delegated by the proposed Constitution to the federal government are few and defined. Those which are to remain in the state governments are numerous and indefinite."[8]**

The settlement reached between the Federalists and the Anti-Federalists was based on the idea that federal government would supplement the states in areas they were not equipped to handle. Neither side envisioned an America where the federal government's reach would extend into practically every nook and cranny of state and local government.

If the Anti-Federalists were alive to witness the state of affairs in the U.S. today, they would likely start tossing crates of tea into the Atlantic Ocean all over again. In truth, the Federalists themselves would probably join them.

Here are a few examples of federal encroachment on state law:

Family law is a state issue and always has been. Marriage, divorce, adoption, and related matters vary from state to state. For example, some states have very traditional views on divorce, making it difficult to achieve. Other states are quick to dissolve a marriage.

However, the federal government has become increasingly involved in family law. The Supreme Court recently changed the definition of marriage for all 50 states with its Obergefell v. Hodges decision, which we'll discuss later. With the stroke of a pen, five unelected lawyers set aside the democratic process of voting and decided a heavily debated issue for 320 million Americans.

Health insurance for everyone is now federally mandated. The increase in premiums and deductibles leads Conservatives to argue that nationalized healthcare should be scrapped and we should return this issue to the free market. However, the same rising costs lead Moderns to argue that we should increase federal taxes to pay for this massive government undertaking. In any case, finding Constitutional authority for nationalized health care proves to be an elusive task under the Commerce Clause.

If a man strikes a pregnant woman in the stomach and causes a miscarriage, he can be criminally charged. That's a state issue. Murder is a state issue, as are most crimes. Child abandonment and neglect are also state issues. However, the issue of abortion has been taken over and dominated by the federal government because the Court discovered an unwritten, unmentioned "Right to Privacy" hidden in the shadows of other rights.

The functioning of bathrooms in retail stores and restaurants has always been a local issue. In recent days, however, the federal government has been increasingly vocal and threatening about the need for transsexual-friendly bathrooms. The federal government even threatened to cut funding and take other action against those refusing to comply.

What has happened to the Tenth Amendment and how did we get to this place? Moderns speak dismissively of the Tenth Amendment and argue that Conservatives place too much emphasis on it. Instead, they point to a clause in the Constitution so vague and malleable that it has become known as "The Elastic Clause." Its technical name is the Necessary and Proper Clause. Here's what it says:

> "The Congress shall have power to …

> **make all laws which shall be necessary and proper for carrying into execution the foregoing powers, and all other powers vested by this Constitution in the government of the United States, or in any department or officer thereof."**

The Modern argues federal government has the authority to regulate anything that is "necessary and proper" for the good of the nation. This is essentially a blank check to pass any law in any area about any subject matter, and especially the controversial ones.

Rather than leaving it to the individual states to pass their own laws on highly-debated issues, the federal government now intervenes and passes legislation or issues a Court ruling which has the following effect: Modern states have their laws affirmed while Conservative states have their laws overturned. This pattern has taken place in the areas of abortion, gay marriage, health care, and controversial gender issues.

Most of American culture is built on Judeo-Christian principles and is center-right. However, the Modern approach has the effect of coercing state and local governments to reel awkwardly to the left of center and to get in line with the ruling of an elite Modern minority in Washington D.C.

Another fascinating trend to observe is the Court's fantasy-based interpretation of the Commerce Clause, which gives the federal government the power:

> **"To regulate commerce with foreign nations, and among the several states, and with the Indian tribes."**

The common sense language of this piece of the Constitution fits perfectly with the common sense problem the Founders were having: the colonies were engaging in trade warfare against one another through import and export taxes, and thirteen different colonies trying to negotiate independently with foreign countries was bad for the nation as a whole. It's easy to understand why this was a problem. Imagine if France could negotiate with Georgia and then use that to leverage a better deal with Virginia, then repeat. The Constitution delegated power of international trade and diplomacy to the federal government. It makes sense.

However, despite the narrow purpose behind the Commerce Clause, the federal government has used it to justify passing laws in subject matters wildly beyond its jurisdiction. This is especially true on issues where Conservatives and Moderns deeply disagree, such as gun control. Between 1936 and 1995, the Supreme Court failed to strike down a single federal law as exceeding the scope of the Commerce Clause.

To understand how far out of bounds a federal law has to be in order to be struck down by the Court, consider the extreme facts of the first case to actually fail the

Court's test in the better part of a century: The federal government passed a law attempting to regulate gun-free school zones in all 50 states. A high school kid brought a concealed firearm to class and was criminally charged by federal prosecutors. His attorney challenged the law, arguing that the federal government had no Constitutional authority to regulate gun-free school zones.[9]

The federal prosecutors responded that the law was authorized under the Commerce Clause. Their reasoning? When a kid brings a gun to class it's an "economic activity." How so? Because if lots of kids bring guns to class, all across America, it will inevitably have a major impact on interstate commerce. Got it?

So, for the first time in 60 years, the Court struck down a federal law for overreaching the Commerce Clause. While this result may seem obvious to Conservatives, it was not to the Court, which voted by a precariously tight 5-4 margin to strike it down. A single vote's difference would have upheld the nonsensical law.

I once came face to face with the overreaching Commerce Clause in trial. I was a military prosecutor in Georgia and the defendant was being tried for possession of a large quantity of child pornography. One of the issues the prosecutor has to prove to the judge is that the military court (which is a federal court) has jurisdiction over the case.

In a typical child pornography case, it's easy to establish federal jurisdiction because of the nature of the Internet. In order to commit the crime, the perpetrator has to pull images and videos from all around the country and even the world. In other words, this wasn't just a Georgia crime.[10]

But in addition to being charged with possessing child pornography, this defendant was charged with using his personal computer to create obscene and illicit child sexual material. He made it himself without using the Internet. Was that also a federal crime?

Using the Commerce Clause and federal law, all I had to prove was that any tool used to commit the crime had travelled in interstate commerce. In other words, because his personal computer was manufactured in Texas with parts from California, the crime involved interstate commerce. It was a stretch, I know.

While few Conservatives would recoil at the practice of aggressively prosecuting child molesters and child pornographers, consider that the same argument I used is used in all sorts of federal cases. If part of a gun crosses state lines during its manufacture, sale, or use, then the federal courts can take jurisdiction of the case. In other words, if an Idaho man commits an Idaho crime against an Idaho victim but the weapon was manufactured in New Hampshire, it just became a federal issue.

While it's hard to believe the Justice Department would actually pursue these cases, they often do. Consider the facts of a 2011 case from Ohio: One group of Amish men wanted to humiliate another group of Amish men who they believed were acting hypocritically. As an act of punishment, the attackers forcibly shaved the hair and beards of their victims. The Justice Department filed the case as a hate crime and said they had federal jurisdiction because the hair clippers had been manufactured out of state. This is a real case and this was really their argument.[11]

One of the patterns we see in these cases is the federal government tends to cherry-pick controversial cases and high visibility issues in order to make a statement. In the Amish case, the federal government's goal was to set a precedent for prosecuting religiously motivated "hate crimes." This is a term that opens a Pandora's box of trouble. It paves the way for the federal government criminally prosecuting words (hate speech) and actions (hate crimes) they deem to be reprehensible.

This makes sense when they are prosecuting a KKK member for burning an African American church. It's a totally different story when they target Christians for believing what Christians believe, for saying what Christians say, and for doing what Christians do.

Chapter Four:

<u>Freedom of Religion</u>

Imagine if a person of the Islamic faith wanted the law of the U.S. to reflect values from the Quran. On the other hand, a person of the Jewish faith wanted the law to reflect values from the Torah. The two men get into an argument. They go back and forth but can't seem to agree on a solution. Finally, the Muslim man says he has an idea: "Let's compromise!" he says. "Let's use the Quran!"

Not much of a compromise, is it? In fact, it is essentially like the child who wants to play a game of "I Win" where the only rule is the little brat always wins. The example is absurd, but it's based on how the First Amendment is actually interpreted by our Supreme Court today. The difference is, in real life, the argument isn't between people of the Muslim faith and people of the Jewish faith. Instead, the argument is between people of faith (mainly Christians) on one hand and Moderns on the other.

The Christian voter isn't saying, "The law of America should be Christian because the Bible is right and sinners are wrong!" What he is saying is he has the right to exercise his vote in a republican democracy. Under our system of government, the will of the majority should be reflected in our laws, particularly at the state level.

If Christians happen to be in the majority in a given state, then it follows that the laws of the state will likely reflect Christian values. It isn't a religious theory at all. It's a democratic theory. The same would be true if non-Christians held the majority view.

The Modern responds: "No, the law should not reflect Christian values, even if Christians are in the majority. I have a better idea. Let's compromise. Let's use my values instead!" Not much of a compromise, is it?

Let me show you how we got here. Here is how the Modern argument works: "Christian, you can have your opinions and I can have mine, but please keep your religion to yourself. When we discuss things that affect everyone, like what the law should be, let's keep religion out of it."

Let me introduce you to the concept of "lucky rabbit's foot religion." If you see that someone has a dyed green rabbit's foot hanging by a chain from his wallet, does it offend you? Of course not, because it's merely a silly, superstitious trinket. Although it hangs from the man's wallet, no one expects him to stop and consult his furry friend when he has to make a major life decision. He doesn't bring it up in arguments. It doesn't change who he is or how he votes.

"Lucky rabbit's foot religion" works the same way. A person can be Christian, Muslim, Jewish, or anything else. However, if they agree to carry their values hidden in their back pocket, you'll never be able to tell what they believe. Their faith doesn't impact their speech, their decisions, or their actions.

Consider how C.S. Lewis explained it in "The Screwtape Letters." The book is written from the perspective of a senior demon to a junior demon with advice on how to corrupt a human and tempt him away from God (the Enemy).

> **"Think of your man as a series of concentric circles, his Will being the innermost, his Intellect coming next, and finally his Fantasy. You can hardly hope, at once, to exclude from all the circles everything that smells of the Enemy: but you must keep on shoving all the virtues outward till they are finally located in the circle of Fantasy, and all the desirable qualities inward into the Will. It is only in so far as they reach the Will and are there embodied in habits that the virtues are really fatal to us..."[12]**

Moderns are perfectly happy with lucky rabbit's foot Christians. As long as the Christian's virtues have been pushed outwards into the realm of Fantasy, then there will be no conflict. If the Christian takes his values as seriously as he takes the Easter Bunny, then everyone can get along.

In the middle ground, there are Christians whose virtues are not in the outer circle of Fantasy but have been drawn into the somewhat closer realm of Intellect. This will lead to conflict with the Modern but it is usually half-hearted and over a cup of hot coffee.

At the far extreme, however, are the Christians whose virtues have taken root in their innermost circle of Will. Their thoughts, their speech, and their actions are all guided by their Christian virtues. For these few, the Modern gospel has little to say other than to malign them and declare war upon them.

The magic of the Modern argument is all in the word "Religion." To be more specific, the magic is in how Modern arguments have changed the meaning of the First Amendment. While not the Founding Father's intent, our law currently operates like a series of high concrete walls that attempt to keep different religious groups from overpowering one another. Standing high above the walls is a heavily fortified guard tower. And inside the tower are trained marksmen with scoped rifles. The guards have been ordered to shoot anyone who tries to cross the wall.

"Christianity, stay over there. Judaism, you keep where you are. Islam, don't move past that point." Although the rules are harsh, in theory they sound like they apply equally to everyone.

In real life, however, it doesn't work like this. What

actually happens is organized religion (faith in big "G" God) gets scrutinized, especially Christianity, while competing beliefs in little "g" gods (like humanism, post-modernism, and moral relativism) are invisible to the guard tower. The result: invisible value systems that refuse to call themselves "religion" get to cross back and forth across the wall and dominate culture. A prominent example would be the Modern view that every moral judgment is simply a matter of personal opinion, there are no absolute truths, and to believe otherwise is narrow-minded and bigoted.

The First Amendment states:

> **"Congress shall make no law respecting the establishment of religion, or prohibiting the free exercise thereof..."**

At one time, this meant the U.S. Congress could not create a "Church of the United States" like the British had done with their Church of England. The purpose was to prevent the federal government from interfering with the faith of ordinary Americans. Over the course of time, however, the First Amendment's meaning has entirely changed. Today, it means if the guard tower smells a Christian, it cocks the hammer on the rifle.

There are two clauses here: the Establishment Clause and the Free Exercise Clause. The government is not permitted to establish a state religion, but it is also not allowed to prohibit the free exercise of religion by individuals. There is inherent tension here between these two clauses. Watch how it works:

A student prays a Christian prayer at her public high school graduation. On one hand, if the public school officials let her pray, is the state establishing Christianity as its official religion? On the other hand, if she isn't allowed to pray, is the state prohibiting her from freely exercising her own religion?

A Christian female baker doesn't want to cater a gay wedding based on her religious beliefs. The state sues her business for discrimination. Does that prohibit the baker's free exercise of religion?

A county courthouse has an old statue of the Ten Commandments. Is this the state establishing Judaism or Christianity as state religions?

The Founding Fathers were mostly Christians, and their faith was not incidental to the birth of our nation or to the drafting of our most important document. Moderns are increasingly less interested in what the original intent of the drafters was. Additionally, online articles abound in various attempts to recast these men in the image of the Modern skeptic. Nevertheless, consider these words from the Founding Fathers themselves:

> "While we are zealously performing the duties of good citizens and soldiers, we certainly ought not to be

inattentive to the higher duties of religion. To the distinguished character of patriot, it should be our highest glory to add the more distinguished character of Christian."

–George Washington

"God who gave us life gave us liberty. And can the liberties of a nation be thought secure when we have removed their only firm basis, a conviction in the minds of the people that these liberties are of the gift of God? That they are not to be violated but with His wrath? Indeed, I tremble for my country when I reflect that God is just; that His justice cannot sleep forever; That a revolution of the wheel of fortune, a change of situation, is among possible events; that it may become probable by Supernatural influence! The Almighty has no attribute which can take side with us in that event."

– Thomas Jefferson

> "I have carefully examined the evidences of the Christian religion, and if I was sitting as a juror upon its authenticity I would unhesitatingly give my verdict in its favor. I can prove its truth as clearly as any proposition ever submitted to the mind of man."

– Alexander Hamilton

While the First Amendment was drafted with one purpose in mind, Modern arguments have swayed the Supreme Court far to the left of its original intent. In 1971, the Court struck down a state law that provided for governmental financial support to private school teachers. The argument was that by reimbursing the school for part of the teachers' salaries, the state was establishing Christianity as a state religion.[13]

In 1989, the Court said having a nativity scene in a courthouse was illegal because it was state sponsorship of Christianity. However, the menorah on the courthouse lawn was okay. Why? Because it was sitting next to a Christmas tree. [14]

The result of this was the "Candy Cane rule" where government lawyers scrambled around advising counties and cities to put up secular symbols like candy canes and Christmas trees next to their nativity scenes. If you drowned out the religious message with enough secular noise, you would be safe from the ACLU's lawyers.

In 1992, the Court ruled that a Judeo-Christian prayer offered during a public school graduation was illegal. Why? Because, they said, the prayer was "coercive" to the other students. Coercion is defined as "the use of force or intimidation to obtain compliance." The Court's argument was that a student who was neither Christian nor Jewish would be forced to hear the offensive prayer and it might be psychologically damaging or inconvenient for them.[15]

To this madness, no one provides a better dose of sanity than the late Justice Antonin Scalia, who said in his fiery dissent that the Court's opinion was suspiciously lacking any support from American history. In his words:

> **"[The Court's decision] lays waste a tradition that is as old as public school graduation ceremonies themselves, and that is a component of an even more longstanding American tradition of nonsectarian prayer to God at public celebrations generally…"**
>
> **Today's opinion shows more forcefully than volumes of argumentation why our Nation's protection, that fortress which is our Constitution, cannot possibly rest upon the changeable philosophical predilections of the Justices of this Court, but must have deep foundations in the historic**

> practices of our people...
>
> The Court's argument that state officials have "coerced" students to take part in the invocation and benediction at graduation ceremonies is, not to put too fine a point on it, incoherent..."

The Founders would never have intended such a postmodern reading of the First Amendment as the majority opinion suggests. Consider that the day after Congress passed the First Amendment, they established "a national day of prayer and thanksgiving," which we of course know today as Thanksgiving. Might it one day be argued that letting out schools and closing government offices on Thanksgiving is an illegal act of state-sanctioned religion? After all, who are we giving thanks to if not God?

In contrast to the strict scrutiny directed towards Christianity, consider how the Modern gospel is preached on every corner. The values of political correctness, moral relativism, and secular humanism are marketed freely in public schools and universities without the slightest judicial interference. They simply slip past the guard tower undetected.

"The First Amendment doesn't apply," the Modern argues. "We merely teach philosophy, history, and other secular studies. We are not a religion." But what is a religion if not a total value system with beliefs and sins and blessings and curses, with preachers and lay people, and all the rest? Doesn't Modern thought qualify as a religion itself?

Alright, Christian, what is your proposed solution? Are we to amend the Constitution to make it more religion-friendly? No. All we need to do is to read the words of the Constitution as they're written and not as some would wish them to be.

> **"Congress shall make no law respecting the establishment of religion, or prohibiting the free exercise thereof…"**

Interpreting this doesn't require a degree from Harvard Law. Based on the muddled and confused rulings the Court has given us, it would appear that an Ivy League degree isn't much help, either.

Let's apply the words of the First Amendment to actual Supreme Court cases. The results are predictable, easy to understand, and consistent with what the Founding Fathers intended.

A student prays a Christian prayer at her public high school graduation:

The school clearly isn't establishing Christianity as a state religion. The government isn't forcing anyone to practice the Christian faith. Maybe next year the prayer is from a

Jewish student. The audience should be respectful whether they share the student's faith or not. While it may be inconvenient for a religious minority, learning to be respectful of American traditions and commonly held values is something we should teach students.

Our refusal to do that may explain why we have adults who can't tolerate the differing opinions of others and feel entitled to have the government shut down anyone who disagrees with them for being "bigoted." The argument that hearing the Christian prayer may be psychologically damaging to the non-Christian student is absurd.

A Christian-owned restaurant doesn't want to cater a gay wedding based on their religious beliefs:

The restaurant owners have a right to freely exercise their religion. They are not the government and they are not forcing anything on their customers. If the restaurant doesn't want to serve alcohol because of their faith, they shouldn't have to. The same is true for catering a gay wedding. If Moderns want to boycott the restaurant, that is perfectly legal. But the government should have no role in punishing, humiliating, or chastising the business.

Just because the business owners have committed a cardinal sin against the church of the Modern, neither the federal nor state government has any Constitutional authority to lash out against them. Imagine if a Muslim-owned restaurant refused to serve alcohol or pork and they refused to cater a Jewish Bar-Mitzvah. Is it not their right to freely exercise their religion, too? Also consider whether the Moderns would take action against the Muslim restaurant. Of course they wouldn't, because it doesn't fit their hostile narrative against Christians.

A county courthouse has an old statue of the Ten Commandments:

The argument that a Ten Commandments statue is an establishment of government religion defies common sense. Not only is it part of our history and cultural heritage, but it is an unimposing piece of lawn decoration that is incapable of coercing even a fruit fly.

Had the county been founded ages ago by giant Scandanavian warriors who worshipped a mythic sea god, wouldn't we expect to find a Norse statue here and there? The fact that these "Ten Commandments" cases have been heavily litigated is proof that Modern culture has made it a badge of honor to be offended at the slightest provocation. The more deeply and frequently a person is offended, the greater their cultural sensitivity and social intelligence must be.

Chapter Five:

<u>Freedom of Speech</u>

When I was 24 years old, I drove to Valdosta, Georgia, to begin my military service as an Air Force JAG. Being the newest attorney in the office had its perks (When challenged with a difficult legal question, I could always lift my hands in total confusion, known as the "Second Lieutenant salute"), but when it came to case assignments, being the low man on the totem pole was dangerous business. While I did some family and probate law, most of my responsibilities were as a criminal prosecutor.

"Congratulations new guy! Boy do we have a special case for you!"

An Air Force Staff Sergeant had been caught with inappropriate photos while deployed to Iraq. He was apparently taking perfectly legal magazines and cutting out images of small children. He then collected his stash of creepy images in his military duffel bag. Very strange, definitely suspicious, but not a crime. Maybe it was the stress of his deployment, but something caused him to crack. When questioned about the images by customs agents, he gave a full confession to possessing child pornography at his home in the U.S. His addiction was apparently so severe that while deployed to Iraq with restricted Internet access, he had to make due with the magazine cutouts.

As I said, I was based out of Georgia. The Defendant was in Iraq. His unit was physically located back in Texas. My boss flew me out to San Antonio where I sat in a cramped evidence locker room for three days viewing videos that were seized from the Defendant's home. He had accessed child pornography on his home computer. He stalked others' children from the window of his hotel room. He molested his three-year old daughter. And he filmed it all.[16]

During the investigation, I learned so much about a dark world I previously didn't even know existed. The images and videos required me to research what was criminal and what was not. Then I came across a very bizarre ruling.

In 1996, Congress passed the Child Pornography Prevention Act (CPPA).[17] This was a federal law that enforced harsh penalties for possessing, manufacturing, and distributing illicit sexual materials involving minors. Then a group of businesses involved in the adult film and pornography industry sued to have the law struck down as unconstitutional. The Supreme Court ruled that possessing child pornography is only illegal if it is made using actual children.

In other words, if a child is molested and the criminal act is filmed or photographed, it is illegal to possess. However, a class of child pornography known as "virtual" child pornography is perfectly legal to possess because, according to the Court, it is protected speech under the First Amendment.[18]

Virtual child pornography means images and videos of what appear to be minors engaged in sex, but no actual minors were involved in creating the pornography. Sometimes child pornographers create realistic images using advanced technology that are virtually indistinguishable from actual children. They also have the ability to morph the head of a child onto images of adult pornography in a convincing way, tricking the eye. According to the Court, all of this is protected speech under the First Amendment.

Why would the Court bend over backwards to shield this pedophile-inspiring industry? They reasoned virtual child pornography "records no crime and creates no victims" and it is not "intrinsically related" to the sexual abuse of children. The Court rejected the prosecutors' argument that virtual child pornography whets the appetites of child molesters, encourages them to engage in illegal conduct, and provides a tool for them to use in seducing children.

Specifically, the prosecutors were referring to the practice of "grooming" in which an adult perpetrator slowly entices their child victim to engage in sexual acts. A common tactic of pedophiles is to show the child images of child pornography in an attempt to make the sexual activity seem normal and playful.

With the logic only a lawyer could understand (and I

don't mean this as a compliment to my fellow lawyers), the Court decided virtual child pornography was just the artistic expression of the individual, and could not be criminalized.

To the consumer of child pornography, the images are "virtually" the same as actual images, but to the Courts, they are very different. The Court held that the mere tendency of speech to encourage unlawful acts was not a sufficient reason for banning it.

I use this case as a starting point for my discussion of Free Speech in America because I want to show how far Modern thought is willing to bend in order to protect the First Amendment in certain situations.

It strains the limits of a sound mind to believe that the Founding Fathers fought a war against Britain in order to protect pedophile paraphernalia and the tools of its dark industry. Nevertheless, Moderns rose to the war cry and formed a battle line to protect it.

I suppose the Modern argument goes like this: "If we let the stuffy Religious Right criminalize virtual child pornography, what's next? Rated R films? Before long, the morality police will be burning our rock and roll records and forcing us to hold hands and pray together."

Justice Anthony Kennedy, a promoter of Modern thought, said,

"The right to think is the beginning of

> **freedom, and speech must be protected from the government because speech is the beginning of thought."[19]**

In truth, the First Amendment protects nearly anything a person could possibly say. There are very few examples of unprotected speech in America. Examples include shouting "Fire!" in a crowded theater with the intent to cause a riot, or threatening to kill someone. While there has been a lot of discussion lately about "hate speech" even hateful speech is generally protected as well.

On this point, Conservatives and Moderns happen to agree, at least in theory. In practice, however, the two views look very different. In the immigration context, Conservatives frequently say that people who move to our country should assimilate to American values. Moderns retort, "What values, exactly, are American?"

There is no more shining example of an American value than the 'Marketplace of Ideas,' best expressed by Justice Oliver Wendell Holmes.

> **"But when men have realized that time has upset many fighting faiths, they may come to believe even more than they believe the very foundations of their own conduct that the ultimate good desired is better reached by free trade in ideas – that the best test of**

truth is the power of the thought to get itself accepted in the competition of the market, and that truth is the only ground upon which their wishes safely can be carried out."[20]

[Simplified translation: Rather than silencing one another, getting offended, or name-calling, we should welcome open debate with those we disagree with. The best idea will eventually win.]

Interestingly, it is now Conservatives who are the champions of Free Speech and Moderns who are made uneasy by opposing ideas. If the Marketplace of Ideas theory is worth an ounce of blood, and our soldiers have spilled an ocean, then Americans should be free to engage one another with differing opinions without the nannying or bullying of the government.

Strictly speaking, the First Amendment applies only to the government and not to private actors. Take the Chick-Fil-A case for example. The CEO of a business stated that he believed in the traditional definition of marriage. There were two Modern reactions: First, thousands boycotted the restaurant chain. Second, government officials in left-leaning cities made public statements that they would use their zoning power to keep the restaurant chain out.[21]

The CEO's statement was protected Free Speech. So

was the boycott. If you don't like his views, you don't have to buy his chicken. But on the other hand, mayors threatening to push out the restaurant using zoning ordinances? Now that's illegal. Rather than engaging the CEO in the Marketplace of Ideas with a different viewpoint, they simply wanted to silence him using the machinery of government.

The First Amendment only restricts government censorship of ideas. It doesn't strictly apply when private actors such as businesses and civilian protestors engage in censorship. However, a great debate is ongoing in America about the importance of Free Speech and whether we are a society that is truly committed to the Marketplace of Ideas.

It appears that the Modern view of Free Speech has become increasingly qualified: You have the right to speak freely, so long as your speech does not offend the pillars of Modern thought. If the speech violates this condition, it is not Free Speech to be protected but is "Hate Speech" to be silenced. The Modern censor labels the offending thoughts as racist, sexist, homophobic, trans-phobic, or the lazier but more generally applied "bigoted." As the Secretary General of the Council of Europe said, "Hate Speech is not Free Speech."[22]

Consider some examples of Modern censorship of Free Speech:

A Conservative speaker who is invited

by a student group is cancelled by the university due to concerns about the "well-being" of the students;[23]

A neurosurgeon is bullied into cancelling his graduation speech at his alma mater because students were offended by his support of traditional marriage;[24]

Protestors are trained, funded, and transported to riots in order to achieve media notoriety on hot button leftist issues.[25]

Litigants claim to be offended by Christian prayers in order to sue schools;[26]

Litigants claim to be offended by Judeo-Christian monuments in order to sue counties;[27]

Litigants claim to be offended by Christian businesses in order to establish anti-gay discrimination lawsuits;[28]

While most of these Modern responses are not government action and few invoke the First Amendment strictly speaking, all have the intended effect of chilling Conservative speech. In the not too distant past, groundless allegations of racism, sexism, or homophobia were enough to end a person's career. In many places, that's still the case.

Finally, a word on "hate speech." This is a term that has taken on a life of its own in recent years. At one time it was a generic term for someone spouting the "N" word at a group of African Americans. But to Moderns, it now means much, much more than this.

In Europe and even as nearby as Canada, Christians have been criminally prosecuted by the government for the "hate speech" of quoting Bible verses on homosexuality and expressing the view that homosexuality is an immoral lifestyle.[29]

In the U.S. the government has fined Christian business owners for not catering to gay weddings, essentially putting them out of business.[30] In the past, the government would put people in jail for not paying their debts (thus the term "debtor's prison"). Now the government can shut down your private business because they think your religious beliefs are "hateful" by whatever standards they use, and from whatever source their standards come. If your convictions in "big G" God offend the strictures of their "little g" gods, you better have a good lawyer.

Chapter Six:

Freedom of the Press

The First Amendment states that Congress shall make no law abridging the Freedom of the Press. In fact, the press has special protections in America because of their sacred responsibility to tell the truth and keep the government honest. Some have referred to the press as "the Fourth Estate" or the fourth branch of government because of its ability to check and balance the Legislative, Executive, and Judicial branches.

However, a compelling case can be made that at this time in history, the press is largely failing at its appointed task and has instead become the public relations office for those on the political left. But biased reporting is not a new problem. Consider this quote by Thomas Jefferson:

> "The most effectual engines for [pacifying a nation] are the public papers... [A despotic] government always [keeps] a kind of standing army of newswriters who, without any regard to truth or to what should be like truth, [invent] and put into the papers whatever might serve the ministers. This suffices with the mass of the people who have no means of distinguishing the false from the true

paragraphs of a newspaper."[31]

[Simplified translation: The way a manipulative government controls the population is through the media. It doesn't matter if what they report is true, so long as it pushes the right agenda.]

After the 2016 Presidential election, the credibility of the mainstream media took a major blow. Most of the press was highly partisan and one-sided in their coverage of the election. Further aggravating the problem was the media's apparent need to shout from the rooftops how objective and neutral they were. The trend of "fact-checking" came into vogue, which is the practice of a partisan reporter pretending to be a disinterested bean counter, merely calculating data points. The impression left by such "neutral" stories, however, is strongly one-sided. The endless number of these types of stories is an insult to the intelligence of the American citizen.

Imagine if newspapers were color-coded based on their political viewpoint. What if the Conservatives produced a red newspaper and the Moderns produced a blue one. The two sides would write about the same stories, based on the same facts, but the content would be totally different. It would be like listening to two opposing lawyers argue their case to a jury.

What I appreciate about this approach is that the writer acknowledges up front what his viewpoint is. He's honest. He's conscious of his bias and doesn't try to hide it. This gives the reader an opportunity to take his words for what they're worth. A Conservative could pick up a blue newspaper and know exactly what he's reading.

Instead, our black-and-white newspapers all claim to be neutral and yet are not. The individual writers have political axes to grind and the companies that own the media have clear ideological leanings one way or the other.

(It's mostly one way and not so much the other, by the way.) When challenged, the press responds with righteous indignation: "There are no red facts or blue facts. There are only facts. We report the facts."

Of course we know this is nonsense. As a young lawyer I learned the difference between an opening statement and a closing argument. In an opening statement, the lawyer can only recite facts. No opinions or arguments are permitted.

"My client, the plaintiff, was parked behind the stop sign. The defendant was going 20 miles per hour over the posted speed limit when his car struck my client's car." These are facts, not opinions.

By contrast, in closing argument the attorney can draw conclusions from the facts and make his case for why the jury should agree with his side.

"My client was innocently sitting at the stop sign praying about the starving children in Africa when the defendant came flying in like a demon and recklessly crushed my client's car to pieces!"

Although the lawyer is only permitted to use facts during the opening statement and is not permitted to "argue," is he being neutral and objective or is he taking a side and trying to persuade the jury? The answer is clear.

An experienced lawyer knows that the opening statement is perhaps the greatest opportunity he will ever get to "argue" his case. How? The same way the press shapes the news stories. Facts can be emphasized or de-emphasized. Facts can be rearranged and placed in a convincing order of events. Facts can be organized to leave a desired impression. How a story is told can make all the difference in the world. And all the better if it seems like the advocate is being neutral and stating "just the facts."

The press loses a lot of credibility by pretending neutrality that isn't really there. Imagine if the attorneys in our car wreck case did the same thing. What if the Plaintiff's lawyer starting prattling on about how he didn't really care who won, but he was just in pursuit of the facts. A jury with any common sense would never buy it. The Plaintiff's lawyer represents one side and the Defense lawyer represents the other. Let's not pretend otherwise.

Since the 2016 Presidential election, a common refrain among Moderns is that the election was influenced because of Conservative "fake news." Modern media giants are making furious attempts to equate Conservative news outlets to conspiracy-theory tabloids. Let me explain the weight of this accusation.

The press is protected under the First Amendment as long as what they report is factually true. Libel and slander lawsuits fall apart when the press is merely reporting the truth. If, on the other hand, they are reporting lies, they fall outside the scope of Constitutional protection.

Looking a few moves ahead on the chessboard, the Modern strategy appears to be this: First, label Conservative media outlets as "fake" to discredit them. Second, censor them through private businesses like social media platforms. Third, censor them using the government.

Private censorship has already begun, as Facebook has hired outside "fact-checkers" to label certain news stories as unreliable.[32] By their own description, the program is only in its "pilot" stage and is focusing on the "worst offenders." Where it goes from here is unfortunately predictable. Government censorship can take place in the form of regulations, tax treatment, libel and slander lawsuits, and even criminal prosecution for hate speech.

Chapter Seven:
Redefining Marriage

Conservatives believe that American society is built from the bottom up. That is, from the family to the community and from the community to the state. The family works to provide food, clothing, housing, and medical care for its members. Government involvement is to be limited. The belief that the family is the fundamental building block of society goes back to Aristotle and beyond.[33]

Critically, the family is the primary way one generation passes along culture to the next generation. Despite the Modern monopoly on media and entertainment in America today, the tremendous influence of Modern thought is muffled by the consistent staying power of the everyday American family.

The Modern view of society, however, works from the top-down. At the top is the powerful federal government. At the bottom is the individual. Everything in between is less important. The traditional family structure is more fluid. The government provides benefits. The benefits are paid for with taxes. As the benefits increase, the taxes increase. The extreme form of this is Socialism, in which the federal government replaces the father and mother as the provider in every sense.

Conservatives believe individual states should operate as independent "Laboratories of Democracy." In other words, New Hampshire might do it a little differently than Virginia, and that's okay. One state wants an 80 mile-per-hour speed limit on its highways while another prefers to lower it to 65. One state legalizes marijuana while another makes it a crime to possess. One state gives murderers therapy while another state sticks a needle in their arm.

Family law works the same way. This is an area of the law that has always been left to the individual states. As expected, the states' approach to marriage is unique.

Take "covenant" marriage, for example, which exists in Arkansas, Louisiana, and Arizona. Under this type of marriage, pre-marital counseling is required and the grounds for divorce are limited. In contrast, obtaining a divorce in most other states is a quick and streamlined process.

If the majority of voters in covenant marriage states want to abolish it, they have the right to do so. If the majority of voters in non-covenant marriage states wish to try it out, they also have that right.

The difference between these two approaches to marriage and divorce is a reflection of the values of the voters in those states. This is how a democratic republic is supposed to work.

Before June 26, 2015, the gay marriage debate was a

living example of the "Laboratories of Democracy" ideal working itself out in real life. Of the 50 states, 11 had voted to redefine marriage to include same-sex couples. Most states, however, chose to keep the traditional definition of marriage.

When the democratic process of voting proved unfavorable, however, multiple same-sex couples pursued a different strategy: they petitioned the Supreme Court. In <u>Obergefell v. Hodges</u>, five Justices took the issue away from the states and decided that gay marriage would be the law of the land for 320 million Americans.[34]

The Court started its analysis with the 14th Amendment, which says that no state shall:

> **"... deprive any person of life, liberty, or property, without due process of law; nor deny to any person within its jurisdiction the equal protection of the laws."**

The key clause mentioned here is the Due Process Clause. The Court said that in addition to protecting "enumerated" rights (which are expressly listed in the Constitution such as the Right to Free Speech), Due Process also protects several un-enumerated, or unmentioned rights. In order for an un-enumerated right to be protected by the Constitution, it has to be "fundamental" or something that is deeply rooted in American history and tradition.

If a proposed right is not deeply rooted in our history and tradition, then it's not fundamental. The purpose of this rule is to prevent a handful of Justices from substantially changing society based on their own personal views by "discovering a fundamental right" that happens to align with their own values.

Here, the slim 5-4 majority of the Court unilaterally tossed all that out the window. "History and tradition guide and discipline this inquiry but do not set its outer boundaries," they state. Instead, the Court can now use its own "reasoned judgment" to discover fundamental rights that no one has recognized before, such as the right for an adult to marry another adult of the same gender.

In fact, the Court says its "new insight" into liberty "as we learn its meaning" has revealed to them that gay marriage is a new right that must be addressed.

The Chief Justice, who strongly disagreed with the majority, explains why this is unwise:

> **"Allowing unelected federal judges to select which un-enumerated rights rank as 'fundamental' – and to strike down state laws on the basis of that determination – raises obvious concerns about the judicial role. Our precedents have accordingly insisted that judges 'exercise the utmost care'**

in identifying implied fundamental rights, 'lest the liberty protected by the Due Process Clause be subtly transformed into the policy preferences of the Members of this Court.'"

The Achilles' Heel of the majority's argument is apparent: if the newly discovered right to marry means any consenting adult can marry any consenting adult, then why can't a consenting adult marry two other consenting adults? In other words, if the Court can redefine marriage to include two people of the same-sex, why can't they redefine marriage to include three people?

In fact, polygamous marriages have been much more widely accepted throughout history than same-sex relationships. The first time same-sex marriage was ever legally recognized was in 2000 in The Netherlands. Polygamous marriages, by contrast, go back thousands of years.

If the Due Process Clause ensures the "Right to Marriage" is a "fundamental" right then surely it must also apply to groups of three? As Justice Roberts noted in his dissent, "If the majority is willing to take the big leap, it is hard to see how it can say no to the shorter one." At the time of the Court's decision, it was estimated that there were half a million "polyamorous" families in the United States. The Modern community was already clamoring for the "Constitutional Right to Plural Marriage."

Separate from the Due Process Clause, the majority also said the Equal Protection Clause requires that states authorize same-sex marriage. They provided no legal analysis for this critical ruling except to say that there is "synergy" between the Due Process Clause and the Equal Protection Clause working together. In Equal Protection decisions going back 150 years, the legal analysis is detailed, methodical, and precise. Not so here. Like a cell phone commercial, the Court simply alludes to "synergy" and then moves on.

Justice Scalia points out the majority's intellectual sloppiness in his dissent:

> **"The world does not expect logic and precision in poetry or inspirational pop-philosophy; it demands them in the law. The stuff contained in today's opinion has to diminish this Court's reputation for clear thinking and sober analysis."**

The majority ends the opinion by promising that those who disagree with gay marriage on religious grounds will be protected by the First Amendment. This promise is little comfort to the Oregon couple that was later fined $135,000 by the government for refusing to bake a gay wedding cake on religious grounds.[35] On that case, the Court has been silent.

Ultimately, however, the biggest Constitutional problem

with the <u>Obergefell</u> decision is that the Supreme Court had no reason to intrude upon the democratic processes of the states. Family law is a state issue and always has been. Marriage, along with divorce, child custody, alimony, and all the rest of it, is left to the states. That's why it's harder to get a divorce in Arkansas than it is in California. How families are defined, and how marriage is defined, should be left to the individual states to decide.

So how would this whole "Laboratories of Democracy" idea work out practically? Imagine an America where Texas recognizes only traditional marriage, while New York allows traditional and gay marriage, and California allows any adult to marry any adult for any reason. I believe this to be what the Founders intended and a much fairer representation of a democratic republic. In contrast, <u>Obergefell</u> has set the precedent that when a majority of the Court feels strongly about a social issue, they will contort the Constitution to whatever political end is desired, all while paying lip service to the importance of liberty and our democratic form of government.

Chapter Eight:

<u>Abortion</u>

In the famous story *The Wizard of Oz*, a group of odd travellers makes its way along a dangerous journey in search of a magical, all-powerful wizard. In the end, they find him. But there's a problem. He's not magical, he isn't all-powerful, and he isn't even a wizard! Behind the curtain, it's just a little man pulling levers and blowing smoke.

We tend to view the Supreme Court like a group of mighty wizards who conjure up the meaning of the Constitution through their towering intellect and inspired reason. After practicing law for a decade, however, I've come to the conclusion that behind the curtain there are only mortals: men and women who make rulings largely based on their own political viewpoints.

My Constitutional Law professor explained it like this: Our Supreme Court Justices sound a lot like a familiar character from *Through the Looking Glass* by Lewis Carroll. Humpty Dumpty was having an argument with Alice about the meaning of the word, "glory."

> "When I use a word," Humpty Dumpty said, in rather a scornful tone, "it means just what I choose it to mean – neither more nor less." "The

question is," said Alice, "whether you can make words mean so many different things."[36]

The role of the Judiciary is not to make law, but to interpret it. But make no mistake; the power to interpret is the power to create, to expand, and to destroy. Or at least, it can be.

While entire books have been written on the legal issues associated with abortion, I will keep my discussion brief. I only intend to lift back the curtain enough for common sense to reveal that there is no wizard behind the curtain: only politics masquerading as law.

While some of the details have changed, the centerpiece of abortion law in America is still <u>Roe v. Wade</u>. In that case, a pregnant single woman (Roe) challenged a Texas law restricting abortion.[37] The law made it a crime to get an abortion unless the life of the mother was in danger.

The Court, as we know, struck down the Texas law as unconstitutional. So what was their basis for taking the case to begin with, and why was the abortion issue removed from the states?

As we discussed earlier during the example of lawyers giving opening statements, it is crucial how an issue is framed. How the story is told and what vocabulary is chosen can make all the difference.

Conservatives frame the issue of abortion like this: There

are two lives involved. The mother has an interest in her own safety, well-being, and convenience. But the unborn child also has an interest: its very life.

The Court, however, dismissed this. Instead of weighing the interest of the mother with the interest of the child, they quickly and summarily stated that a fetus is not a "person" under the 14th Amendment. That's it. There's no meaningful legal analysis, no detailed medical discussion, nothing. They simply state, "The Constitution does not define 'person' in so many words."

And without even the appearance of thoughtful consideration, the issue was permanently decided: an unborn child is not a person and has no Constitutional rights at all. Under this logic, thirty minutes before a newborn infant is crying in the arms of its mother, it is not a person. From a legal standpoint, it's simply biological material. The hypocrisy of this position is evident when considering that a criminal defendant who kills a pregnant woman can be charged with the deaths of both "persons." Additionally, if the woman were to kill her child thirty seconds after it is born, she can be charged with murder. If she fails to care for it, she can be charged with child abandonment or neglect.

But you don't get to become a Supreme Court Justice by being a dummy, and there's a brilliant reason why the Court quickly sidesteps the issue of what rights the unborn child has. If the Court were to recognize the child as a person, then the 14th Amendment would kick in. Remember this?

> **"... nor shall any state deprive any person of life, liberty, or property, without due process of law; nor deny to any person within its jurisdiction the equal protection of the laws."**

What would happen to <u>Roe v. Wade</u> if the Court had to apply Due Process and Equal Protection guarantees to the life of an unborn child? Abortion would be illegal nationwide at the earliest opportunity. When the Modern position would lose the legal analysis, it appears that their strategy is to avoid the legal analysis altogether.

Instead of framing the issue like professional legal scholars should, the Court framed it like the work of bad poets or amateur philosophers: does the Constitution give a woman a Right to Privacy in her body, and does that Right to Privacy include the right to terminate her pregnancy?

The way the issue is framed is preposterous, and bears no relation to logic, common sense, or Constitutional precedent. What does the issue of abortion have to do with privacy? And if the child is a person, then what does privacy matter anyway? Our criminal laws authorize invasive searches of homes and bodies pursuant to a warrant in simple drug cases. If the law sometimes permits the invasion of a person's privacy in order to find a few ounces of methamphetamine, then why is the issue foreclosed when a potential life is at stake?

In any case, once we accept that the issue has been framed by the Court in an absurd manner, let's continue. Where in the Constitution, exactly, is this Right to Privacy?

Justice Blackmon, the author of the majority opinion, explains:

> **"The Constitution does not explicitly mention any right of privacy."**

[Simplified translation: It isn't there.]

But the legal wizardry has only just begun. Not only is the vague and ill defined Right to Privacy not in the Constitution, but the Court proudly states, with a wink, that the right to abortion is hidden "in the penumbras of the Bill of Rights." (A penumbra is essentially a shadow.)

So to summarize, the Court rules that abortion is now legal in all 50 states because a woman has a Right to Privacy which isn't mentioned in the Constitution and is hidden in the shadows of other rights and this Right to Privacy means the right to kill her unborn child because it isn't a person but is merely biological material. Understood?

The Court finds that the woman's right to an abortion is a "fundamental" right under the 14th Amendment, but it was never mentioned in the Constitution. Under its own precedent and case law, in order for a right be "fundamental" it has to be "so rooted in the traditions and conscience of our people as to be ranked fundamental." This means the tradition and history of the country at the time of the 14th Amendment should be considered.

At the time the 14th Amendment was passed in 1868, at least 36 states had laws on the books restricting abortion. The Court's ruling in Roe v. Wade made the wild assertion that the people who enacted the 14th Amendment and those who lived and died from 1868 until 1973 were simply too blind to see the secret abortion right hiding behind a penumbra shadow in the corner. Justice Blackmon's majority, however, had the legal brilliance to summon the buried right from its shadowy hiding place and into the light of day for the first time. Understood?

Unlike gay marriage, which I believe is an issue that should be decided state-by-state under the 10th Amendment, abortion could very well be a federal issue because the unborn child should be recognized as a 'person' with Due Process and Equal Protection rights under the Constitution.

However, if the Court is unwilling to dignify the unborn with the extravagant compliment of 'personhood' then they should remove themselves from the highly contentious, heavily debated subject altogether and leave it to the democratic processes of the individual states.

Words have meaning, and when the Constitution doesn't say it, it isn't there. Our Courts have been playing Humpty Dumpty for far too long and it is their duty to have the integrity to abstain from making legal rulings far outside their scope of authority.

Conclusion

I wrote this book as the first in a series of short pieces on our Constitution, laws, and government. My hope is after reading this, the reader will be frustrated in a sense by the lack of volume in these pages.

How could a Texan write a book on the U.S. Constitution and not talk about guns? What about immigration? If I've achieved anything at all, I've achieved a work of incompleteness. But this will have to do for now.

The reader has my sincere appreciation for their patience. My hope is that this book has strengthened your convictions. May you be encouraged to think and speak freely, clearly, lovingly, and fearlessly.

Appendix:

The Bill of Rights and the 14th Amendment

Amendment I

Congress shall make no law respecting an establishment of religion, or prohibiting the free exercise thereof; or abridging the freedom of speech, or of the press; or the right of the people peaceably to assemble, and to petition the government for a redress of grievances.

Amendment II

A well-regulated militia, being necessary to the security of a free state, the right of the people to keep and bear arms, shall not be infringed.

Amendment III

No soldier shall, in time of peace be quartered in any house, without the consent of the owner, nor in time of war, but in a manner to be prescribed by law.

Amendment IV

The right of the people to be secure in their persons, houses, papers, and effects, against unreasonable searches and seizures, shall not be violated, and no warrants shall issue, but upon probable cause, supported by oath or affirmation, and particularly describing the place to be searched, and the persons or things to be seized.

Amendment V

No person shall be held to answer for a capital, or otherwise infamous crime, unless on a presentment or indictment of a grand jury, except in cases arising in the land or naval forces, or in the militia, when in actual service in time of war or public danger; nor shall any person be subject for the same offense to be twice put in jeopardy of life or limb; nor shall be compelled in any criminal case to be a witness against himself, nor be deprived of life, liberty, or property, without due process of law; nor shall private property be taken for public use, without just compensation.

Amendment VI

In all criminal prosecutions, the accused shall enjoy the right to a speedy and public trial, by an impartial jury of the state and district wherein the crime shall have been committed, which district shall have been previously ascertained by law, and to be informed of the nature and cause of the accusation; to be confronted with the witnesses against him; to have compulsory process for obtaining witnesses in his favor, and to have the assistance of counsel for his defense.

Amendment VII

In suits at common law, where the value in controversy shall exceed twenty dollars, the right of trial by jury shall be preserved, and no fact tried by a jury, shall be otherwise reexamined in any court of the United States, than according to the rules of the common law.

Amendment VIII

Excessive bail shall not be required, nor excessive fines imposed, nor cruel and unusual punishments inflicted.

Amendment IX

The enumeration in the Constitution, of certain rights, shall not be construed to deny or disparage others retained by the people.

Amendment X

The powers not delegated to the United States by the Constitution, nor prohibited by it to the states, are reserved to the states respectively, or to the people.

Amendment XIV (Section 1)

All persons born or naturalized in the United States, and subject to the jurisdiction thereof, are citizens of the United States and of the state wherein they reside. No state shall make or enforce any law which shall abridge the privileges or immunities of citizens of the United States; nor shall any state deprive any person of life, liberty, or property, without due process of law; nor deny to any person within its jurisdiction the equal protection of the laws.

About the Author

Clay Harrison is a native of Sulphur Springs, Texas. He is the son of Dr. Juan and Mrs. Sheri Harrison. After graduating from high school in 2002, he attended the University of Texas at Austin on an Air Force ROTC scholarship. He graduated from college and commissioned as a military officer at age 20 before attending law school at Baylor University on an academic scholarship. He joined the Air Force JAG Corps at 24 and served for four years in Georgia, Okinawa, and other locations.

During his military service, he was deployed to the tropical island of Mindanao in the Philippines in support of counterinsurgency operations against the Abu Sayyaf ("Bearer of the Sword") terror group. The Abu Sayyaf organization made its reputation as a particularly violent jihadist threat in the southern Philippines, specializing in kidnapping for ransom operations.

As the lone attorney for a joint special operations unit of Navy SEALs, Army Special Forces, and other combat soldiers, he advised military commanders on the law of war and rules of engagement as well as numerous civil law issues. He also directed an intelligence program that rewarded Filipino civilians for providing information on high value enemy targets.

He separated honorably from the Air Force in the summer of 2012 in order to return home to Texas. In

2013 he wrote <u>The Great and Terrible Wilderness</u>, a novel, and made the transition from military JAG to civilian prosecutor.

Clay and his wife Tara lead the Crossover young adult ministry at The Way Bible Church and are expecting their first child in April. Clay currently serves as an Assistant District Attorney for Hopkins, Franklin, and Delta Counties.

Notes

[1] http://www.washingtonexaminer.com/media-agree-trans-bathroom-laws-are-the-new-jim-crow/article/2591843
[2] *The Weight of Glory*, by C.S. Lewis
[3] *Orthodoxy*, by G.K. Chesterton
[4] *God in the Dock*, by C.S. Lewis
[5] The Declaration of Independence
[6] Benjamin Franklin's Request for Prayers at the Constitutional Convention
[7] *U.S. Foreign Policy and the (Blessed) Pains of Checks and Balances* by George Friedman
[8] *The Federalist #45*
[9] US v. Lopez, 514 U.S. 549
[10] US v. Hogeland, ACM 37821 (Air Force Court of Criminal Appeals)
[11] https://www.cir-usa.org/cases/u-s-v-miller/
[12] *The Screwtape Letters*, by C.S. Lewis
[13] Lemon v. Kurtzman, 403 U.S. 602 (1971)
[14] Allegheny County v. Greater Pittsburgh ACLU, 492 U.S. 573 (1989)
[15] Lee v. Weisman, 505 U.S. 577 (1992)
[16] U.S. v. Haley, ACM 37565 (Air Force Court of Criminal Appeals)
[17] 18 U.S.C. Section 2252A
[18] Ashcroft v. Free Speech Coalition, 535 U.S. 234 (2002)
[19] Ashcroft v. Free Speech Coalition, 535 U.S. 234 (2002)
[20] Abrams v. United States, 250 U.S. 616 (1919)
[21] http://www.cnn.com/2012/07/30/opinion/randazza-first-amendment/
[22] https://www.coe.int/en/web/portal/-/hate-speech-is-not-free-speech-says-secretary-general-ahead-of-human-rights-day
[23] https://www.insidehighered.com/news/2016/10/21/several-universities-cancel-appearances-conservative-writer-milo-yiannopoulos

24 https://www.washingtonpost.com/lifestyle/style/commencement-speaker-protests-stir-a-debate-over-free-speech-on-campuses/2013/04/11/a5b4914e-a2da-11e2-82bc-511538ae90a4_story.html?utm_term=.d1520da099c8
25 http://www.foxnews.com/us/2016/11/10/trump-protests-intensify-as-doubts-swirl-about-spontaneity.html
26 Lee v. Weisman
27 Allegheny County v. Greater Pittsburgh ACLU
28 http://www.cnn.com/2016/11/15/politics/oregon-bakery-official-lost-trnd/
29 Europe and Canada prosecuting Christians
30 http://www.cnn.com/2016/11/15/politics/oregon-bakery-official-lost-trnd/
31 Jefferson quote number two
32 http://www.npr.org/2016/12/18/506045492/employing-third-party-fact-checking-facebook-unveils-new-plan-to-curb-fake-news-
33 *The Politics*, Aristotle
34 Obergefell v. Hodges, 576 U.S. ___ (2015)
35 http://www.usnews.com/news/articles/2015-12-30/sweet-cakes-bakery-owners-in-oregon-pay-fine
36 *Through the Looking Glass*, by Lewis Carroll
37 Roe v. Wade, 410 U.S. 113 (1973)